W W M D

What Would Marianne Do?

QUOTES TO LIVE BY

APOLLO
PUBLISHERS

Apollo Publishers books may be purchased for educational, business, or sales promotional use. Special editions may be made available upon request. For details, contact Apollo Publishers at info@apollopublishers.com.

Visit our website at www.apollopublishers.com.

Published in compliance with California's Proposition 65.

Library of Congress Cataloging-in-Publication Data is available on file.

Front cover illustration by Lady Jday, https://ladyjday.com.
Cover composition, back cover, and interior design by Rain Saukas.

Print ISBN: 978-1-948062-54-1
Ebook ISBN: 978-1-948062-55-8

Printed in the United States of America.

CONTENTS

LOVE

Romance is one of the
sacred temples that dot
the landscape of life.

"

The way to get over someone
breaking your heart is to visualize
yourself pouring buckets of
divine love all over them.

"

"

Our greatest power to
effect visible things lies in
understanding some invisible
things. Only love—not money or
machines—moves mountains.

"

"

We are not held back by the love we did not receive in the past but by the love we're not extending in the present.

"

"

The daughters of God
don't brake for jerks.

"

"

Any time you try to be a
loving person, you are doing
your part to save the world.

"

Love is all around us all
the time. Love is the ethers
that we swim in. Love is the
amniotic fluid of the soul.

"

Love is the intuitive
knowledge of our hearts.

"

"

If I choose to bless another
person, I will always end up
feeling more blessed.

"

66

When you're attracted to someone, all that namaste consciousness flies out the window, right?

99

"

The mind wants this
or that, but the heart just
wants to go home.

"

"

Let's all of us give birth to more love in the world today. And then tomorrow too. And then the day after that.

"

> **"**
> Physical circumstances have very little to do with either our capacity to love or attract love.
> **"**

"

There is no Mr. Right
because there is no Mr. Wrong.
There is whoever is in front of
us, and the perfect lessons to
be learned from that person.

"

HEALING
AND
FORGIVENESS

> **"**
> Each of us has a
> unique part to play in the
> healing of the world.
> **"**

Joy is what happens to us when we allow ourselves to recognize how good things really are.

"

Each of us has an inner room
we can visit to be cleansed
of fear-based thoughts and
feelings. This room, the holy of
holies, is a sanctuary of light.

"

"

In every community, there is work to be done. In every nation, there are wounds to heal. In every heart, there is the power to do it.

"

> **"**
> Peacock feathers are created
> by peacocks eating thorns.
> Every thorn you have eaten can
> become a peacock feather too.
> **"**

"

The first step in forgiveness
is the willingness to forgive.

"

"

We do not heal the past by
dwelling there; we heal the past
by living fully in the present.

"

A gray sky is actually a blue
sky covered up by gray clouds.
A guilty person is actually
an innocent soul covered
up by mistaken behavior.

> "
> The practice of forgiveness is
> our most important contribution
> to the healing of the world.
> "

"

The goal of spiritual practice
is full recovery, and the only
thing you need to recover from
is a fractured sense of self.

"

“

My self-healing lies in
praying for those who
have harmed me.

”

The cultivation of mental rest, or surrender, is like eating healthy food. It doesn't give us an immediate rush, but over time it provides a lot more energy.

COURAGE

AND

FEARS

> **"**
> Our deepest fear is not that we are inadequate. Our deepest fear is that we are powerful beyond measure. It is our Light, not our Darkness, that most frightens us.
> **"**

> **"**
> Love is what we were born with.
> Fear is what we learned here.
>
> **"**

We can have a grievance or
we can have a miracle, but
we cannot have both.

"

We can always choose to perceive
things differently. You can focus
on what's wrong in your life, or
you can focus on what's right.

"

"

We're hallucinating.
And that's what this world is:
a mass hallucination, where
fear seems more real than love.
Fear is an illusion. Our craziness,
paranoia, anxiety and trauma
are literally all imagined.

"

"

Your job is to allow the Holy Spirit
to remove the fearful thinking
that surrounds your perfect self,
just as excess marble surrounded
Michelangelo's perfect statue.

"

"

As we let our light shine, we
unconsciously give others the
permission to do the same.
As we are liberated from
our own fears, our presence
actually liberates others.

"

"

Dance in the fields
of infinite possibility.

"

GRATITUDE
AND
SELF-ESTEEM

If I were a little less of a Texan
or a little less of a Jew, I might
just give up and go home.

"

Be the most wonderful
expression of you that
you're capable of.

"

The highest form of human intelligence is to observe yourself without judgement.

"

Maturity includes the
recognition that no one
is going to see anything
in us that we don't see in
ourselves. Stop waiting for a
producer. Produce yourself.

"

"

Your playing small does
not serve the world.

"

"

Nothing binds you except
your thoughts; nothing limits you
except your fear; and nothing
controls you except your beliefs.

"

"

We ask ourselves,
'Who am I to be brilliant,
gorgeous, talented, and
fabulous?' Actually, who
are you not to be?

"

"

I was lying awake in my bed worrying
about something when a voice in my
heart said, 'Marianne, most people
in the world do not have beds.'

"

> **"**
> When a woman rises
> up in glory, her energy
> is magnetic and her sense
> of possibility contagious.
> **"**

"

The universe
literally loves you.

"

AGING
AND
GROWTH

"

I remember walking through a store
and I saw clothes a twenty-five-year-old
would wear. And the conversation in my
head was I'm not young and fabulous
anymore. But immediately there was
a voice that said, *No. You can be older
and fabulous.* In other words, still just
as fabulous but in a different way.

"

"

Children are not children.
They are just younger people.
We have the same soul at sixty
that we had at forty, and the same
soul at twenty-five that we had at
five. If anything, children are wiser.

"

"

The world cannot
evolve if girls refuse
to become women.

"

We need love and hugs
just as much as children
need love and hugs.

"

The beauty of personal
authenticity can compensate
for the lost beauty of our youth.
My arms aren't as shapely as
they used to be, but I know so
much more now about what I
should be doing with them.

"

66

I don't know anybody who
doesn't have a lost decade.

99

DIET, HEALTH, AND LIFESTYLE

"

I get that the best lived life
is not 'Well, what do I want to
do today?' The best lived life is,
'How could I be of best use?'

"

"

I have no comfort food.

"

"

It doesn't take money to put on a beautiful robe. It doesn't take a lot of money to put fresh flowers in the house. It doesn't take money to turn off the television and cultivate real bonding time.

"

> ❝
> Charles Manson
> ate apples. That doesn't
> mean I'm not going to.
> ❞

"

Only when you learn to commit
yourself will you stop your
self-sabotaging behavior. It's
not enough just to tell yourself
what not to do; you must learn
a new way to think before you
can learn a new way to be.

"

"

Your relationship to food is but
a reflection to your relationship
to yourself, as is everything in
your life. There's no reason to
think you'll be capable of loyalty
to a diet until you address your
basic disloyalty to yourself.

"

“

People who are meditating every day and involved in a serious spiritual practice don't usually wake up in the morning and want to rush out to eat a bunch of junk food.

”

"

(on the Impossible Burger)

*What is this and why
is it impossible?*

"

"

Turn anxiety and depression
into a sacred journey.

"

> **"**
> I'm a Jewish woman.
> I practice transcendental
> meditation. I do yoga.
>
> **"**

"

God is BIG, swine flu SMALL.
See every cell of your body filled
with divine light. Pour God's
love on our immune systems.

"

"

Love will be
our medicine.

"

"

This entire idea of me as anti-medicine and anti-science could not be further from the truth. I'm a Jewish woman. You could read my last blog, 'I'm a modern woman, of course I go to the doctor.'

"

> **"**
>
> I remember once when
> I was pregnant with my daughter . . .
> sitting there in an easy chair, drinking
> a cup of chamomile tea with my feet
> up on a pillow and thinking to myself,
> *Isn't it interesting, the action I can*
> *take right now that most serves*
> *the process of what is growing*
> *inside me is to simply sit here.*
>
> **"**

I tend to eat little bits throughout the day more than large meals. I'm particularly fond of green grapes.

> **"**
> I've never worn
> a velvet scarf in my life.
> **"**

INDIVIDUALITY
AND
SUCCESS

"

Gay men in LA gave
me my career.

"

"

You can have the best car mechanic in the world, but they're not the one who can necessarily tell you what road you should take.

"

Only do what you feel called
in your heart to do, and then
give all of yourself to the task.

"

The person who can override
someone who is skilled at
luring people into the dark
is someone who is skilled at
luring people into the light.

"

"

The entire universe
is literally conspiring to give
you an amazing day today.
Co-conspire.

"

"

Each of us is pregnant with
a better version of ourselves.

"

"

Listen, in today's world, if they're not killing you, you consider it a good day.

"

"

Your mind is like an airplane,
and YOU are the pilot: Rise
above the clouds. Fly above the
turbulence. Seek a smoother ride.

"

“

I need to learn Spanish
by tomorrow night at 9:00.

”

"

I have a dramatic personality.
If I do things right, it's a big right;
if it's wrong, it's a big wrong.

"

"

I've never felt, nor do I, that
it has ever been my job to
change anyone's perception.
. . . I'm not here to change
anyone, I'm just here to sing the
song that I feel in my heart.

"

"

Everyone feels on some level
like an alien in this world,
because we ARE. We come from
another realm of consciousness,
and long for home.

"

"

Never think you can
separate who you are
from what you're doing.

"

"

If a train doesn't stop
at your station, then
it's not your train.

"

FAITH
AND
SPIRIT

"

I can't believe in the year
2020 that I have to justify the
body mind connection.

"

"

Calling all goddess types: this is a perfect time to do ritualistic nature ceremonies invoking divine alignment between humanity and nature.

"

"

Pray that anyone even thinking of committing a terrorist act, anywhere in the world, be surrounded by a huge golden egg.

"

"
Dear God, Please take
away the swine flu.
Amen.

"

"

Seek ye first the
kingdom of heaven and
the Maserati will get there
when it's supposed to.

"

> **"**
> Religion is like a map.
> The route isn't important.
> It's the destination that matters.
> **"**

If I am a bitch,
I'm a bitch for God.

"

I was always very interested in spiritual topics, starting even when I was a teenager. My mother would always joke about how even when I was a little girl, my prayers would go on for so long.

"

"

Magic is where you ask
the universe to work for you;
miracles is where you ask the
universe what you can do for it.

"

"

I think our chances of a full-scale spiritual wave of power is greater if we keep it to each person's individual schedule. In the quantum realm, time does not matter anyway.

"

> You're a lamp; God is the electricity. You're a faucet; God is the water. You're a human; God is the divine within you. ALLOW the flow.

"

A nervous breakdown is a
highly underrated vehicle for
spiritual transformation.

"

For five minutes a day, be a spiritual activist. You probably already know what to do. Turn off the TV; neither CNN, MSNBC, or FOX knows the news. They only know data. Turn off the bright lights. Put down the newspapers. And go within.

> The holidays are only holy
> if we make them so.

POP
CULTURE
AND
ENTERTAINMENT

> Taylor Swift, you don't
> know me but I sure
> am proud of you.

"

Your screenplay should spread love.
Your hair salon should spread love.
Your agency should spread love.
Movies can be instruments
of enlightenment.

"

> All the films were good but *Avatar* has changed the world. He didn't win an Oscar tonight, but James Cameron deserves a Nobel Peace Prize

"

Saw *Avatar* tonight.
Absolutely unbelievable.
Run, don't walk.

"

If you want a simple explanation
for what's happening in America,
watch *Avatar* again.

"

I do think that *Avatar* told the truth, the whole truth, and nothing but the truth about some very serious socioeconomic realities in our world today. James Cameron was able to transmit such profound truths in cartoon form.

"

> **"**
> I've seen some of the
> most intelligent commentary,
> oddly enough, on memes.
> **"**

"

I've had a personal conversation
with Oprah and I wouldn't
share, I never have.

"

"

(on social media)

The best of things and the worst of things. Like so many other things on the material plane, it's good or bad depending on the purpose ascribed to it by the human mind. This is something

so new, something so
significant and so radical in its
implications, that I think we're just
beginning to have an adequate
understanding of what has
happened and what it means.

POLITICS
AND
CURRENT
AFFAIRS

"

America should be
a golden thread in the
tapestry of the world.

"

"

We need a mother in the White House. We can make history, and we should.

"

> We often talk about less important things because to talk about the most important things would be too emotionally overwhelming. That's why we

aren't having the conversations
we need to be having about
how to create peace; to do
so, we would have to face
the harsh realities of war.

"

I want to be an agent of
change. I don't want to
be an agent of chaos.

"

> **"**
> When was the last time you heard a politician talking about peace on this planet in twenty years? That's why I want to create a Department of Peace.
> **"**

"
Income inequality in America isn't just unethical or immoral; it is unsustainable. Anyone who has read *Yertle the Turtle* already knows this.

"

"

You need someone to
go to Washington who
understands how the mind
of a sociopath works.

"

"

Let's see angels surrounding
the nuclear reactors, pouring
cold water over them, keeping
radiation from escaping
into the atmosphere.

"

"

The power of your mind is greater than the power of nuclear radiation. Visualize angels dispersing it into nothingness.

"

"

We should start sending
light / posting angels around
all polling places now. Massive
forcefield needed to counter
voter intimidation efforts.

"

"

Visualize the oil spills
plugged. Close your eyes for
five minutes and see angels
coming over it, filling it with
sane and sacred thoughts.

"

I don't want shackles.
I don't want chains. Get out
of my face. We want liberty.

"

In other countries they have
two brands of toothpaste and
fourteen presidential candidates;
in America, we have the reverse.

"

The part of a brain that
rationally decides an issue is
not always the side of a brain
that decides who to vote for.

"

Creativity is messy!
Intimacy is messy!
Democracy is messy!
The transition from pure idea
to excellent manifestation has to
go through its chaotic phases.

"

> "
> Just beneath the surface, this isn't politics, it's black magic. Entirely a psychic battle. Use your shield of Virtue and your sword of Truth.
> "

"

Ultimately, what
moves the dial is not
what we fight against
but what we stand for.

"

EGO
AND
HATERS

"

I remind people of
America's mission statements.

"

"

Who am I
not to be President?

"

"

What some people call 'ego,'
I call 'personality.' I have a habit
of saying what I think. That is
a professional strength but
sometimes a personal weakness.

"

"

The world has no idea the power
about to rise from the global
heart. Haters might have guns,
but only lovers have wings.

"

We can take our own lives
seriously, regardless of whether
or not anyone else does.

"

When they go low, go to
a higher frequency where
they cannot touch you.

"

"

When the haters step up the
hate, the lesson for the rest
of us is to step up the love.

"

"

Internal shifts: 1: Try not to hate the haters; otherwise you're just another hater. 2: Honor someone's opinion even if it's not your own. 3: Disagree passionately but without personally demonizing the other.

"

"
When hate shouts, it's not
enough for love to whisper.
"

"

If someone tells you they're being
the devil's advocate, tell them
the devil doesn't need one.

"

This unofficial celebration of the wise words of Marianne Williamson features well-researched quotes sourced from Marianne's spoken word and writing, including on social media. Marianne is a lecturer, activist, nonprofit founder, and author of thirteen books, including *A Return to Love*, *The Law of Divine Compensation*, *The Age of Miracles*, *Enchanted Love*, and *A Politics of Love*. In 2014, Marianne ran as an Independent for California's 33rd congressional district, championing progressive causes including women's rights and LGBTQ equality. She later ran for the Democratic nomination for the 2020 presidential election, officially launching her campaign in January 2019 with her call for a moral awakening. Throughout the course of her campaign, Marianne made waves due to her spiritual zeal and unconventional perspective. A native of Houston, Texas, Marianne resides in Los Angeles, California.